POP CULTURE BIOS

# LOGAN

# LERMAN

## THE PERKS OF BEING AN ACTION STAR

NADIA HIGGINS

Lerner Publications Company

MINNEAPOLIS

Lerner Publications Company
A division of Lerner Publishing Group, Inc.
241 First Avenue North
Minneapolis, MN 55401 USA

For reading levels and more information, look up this title at
www.lernerbooks.com.


Library of Congress Cataloging-in-Publication Data

Higgins, Nadia.
    Logan Lerman : the perks of being of an action star / by
Nadia Higgins.
        p.    cm. — (Pop culture bios)
    Includes index.
    ISBN 978-1-4677-1445-7 (lib. bdg. : alk. paper)
    ISBN 978-1-4677-2501-9 (eBook)
    1. Lerman, Logan, 1992-  —Juvenile literature.  2. Actors—
United States—Biography—Juvenile literature.  I. Title.
PN2287.L4325H55 2014
791.4302'8092—dc23 [B]                        2013025883

Manufactured in the United States of America
1 – PC – 12/31/13

# INTRODUCTION

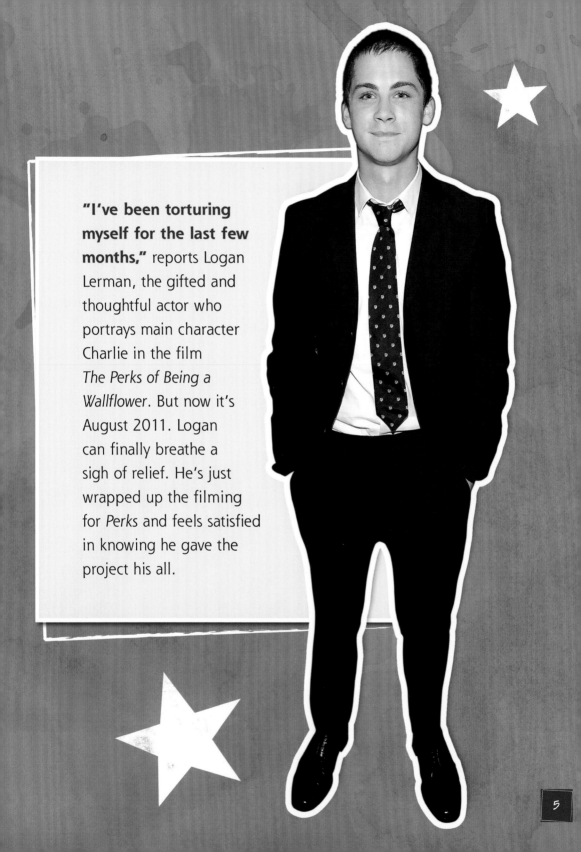

**"I've been torturing myself for the last few months,"** reports Logan Lerman, the gifted and thoughtful actor who portrays main character Charlie in the film *The Perks of Being a Wallflower*. But now it's August 2011. Logan can finally breathe a sigh of relief. He's just wrapped up the filming for *Perks* and feels satisfied in knowing he gave the project his all.

Yet it took a *lot* for Logan to get inside Charlie's head—a lot of prep work, imagination, and thought. And an experience like that doesn't just go away overnight.

"The No. 1 thing for me was isolating myself," Logan says of playing Charlie. He wanted to feel awkward and lonely, just like Charlie. So Logan arrived on set in Pittsburgh, Pennsylvania, two weeks before the rest of the cast. He locked himself in his hotel room. He left only to grab meals—alone—at a nearby T.G.I. Friday's. **"Everyone was looking at me like, 'Poor kid,'"** Logan says, laughing about it now.

They didn't know that nineteen-year-old "kid" was a working actor—an actor preparing for the hardest role

Logan had a lot of fun acting with his costars in *The Perks of Being a Wallflower.*

of his life. And they certainly wouldn't have guessed that Logan was a rising star on the brink of what critics would call his "breakthrough performance."

Of course, Logan himself didn't know that then either. He didn't even know it by August, when filming had wrapped. At that point, he just had that tired-but-happy feeling of completion. As hard as his work had been, Logan had loved every minute of it. And he was proud knowing that he'd faced the challenge with his whole heart and the full force of his actor's imagination.

Logan's mom (LEFT) helped him pursue his dream to become an actor.

# CHAPTER ONE

# AN OBSESSED KID

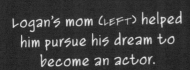

Logan had lots of famous neighbors while growing up in Beverly Hills, California.

"Ardent film geek"—that's how Logan sums himself up on Twitter. That sounds right for a guy whose favorite place is the inside of a movie theater. He could also add "heartthrob," though. Other people do. But that word makes him squirm. "Action hero" is probably okay. And of course, plain old "actor" works too. It's a badge Logan's proudly worn ever since he can remember.

## A Fun Hobby

Logan Wade Lerman was born January 19, 1992, in Beverly Hills, California. His hometown may be a celebrity hot spot. But the Lerman family had nothing to do with show business. In fact, they run a company selling orthotics and prosthetics. ("Braces and fake limbs," Logan explains.)

### LOGAN BASICS

NICKNAME: Loggie
HEIGHT: 5 feet 9 inches (1.8 meters)
FAMILY BACKGROUND: European Jewish
PETS: two dogs

Logan is the youngest of three. His brother, Lucas, is a writer. His sister, Lindsey, designs jewelry. Logan's parents, Larry and Lisa, are divorced. They live close to each other, though. Logan says his family is supertight.

Logan was a pretty normal kid—except for one thing. He _loved_ movies. And not the way every kid loves movies. He first told his parents at the age of two that he wanted to be an actor. Then he just kept begging.

Luckily, in Logan's hometown, auditioning to act was a commonplace activity—not just a far-fetched dream. And his parents had a "why not?" attitude. They thought acting would be a fun hobby for their obsessed son.

Logan hangs out with some of his family members. LEFT TO RIGHT: Lucas; Lindsey; his stepmom, Marilyn Silver; his stepsister, Laura Silver; and Logan.

Logan (LOWER LEFT) turned his movie obsession into a career. His first movie was *The Patriot.*.

## AGENT =
a person whose job it is to help actors find jobs

## A Talented Prop

By the age of four, Logan had an agent. By the time he was seven, he was in a movie. He played the son of Mel Gibson's character in *The Patriot*. That same year, he appeared as a younger version of Mel's character in *What Women Want*.

**"I was just a prop,"** Logan says, laughing about those early roles. He just stood where he was told.

## PROP =
an object, such as a piece of furniture, used on set

But even as a "prop," he managed to shine. The jobs kept coming. In 2003, he landed his first job playing a main character in a movie. He played Luke in the TV thriller *A Painted House*.

## Bad Kid = Musician

Loggie loved getting pulled out of school for a job. He was way too antsy to sit in a classroom. Plus, he was always getting in trouble.

That was true at home too. Logan remembers being grounded a lot. But the punishment was wasted on Logan. He was a homebody anyway. He used that downtime to work on his No. 2 passion—music.

Over the years, Logan would teach himself piano, bass, and guitar. He also dabbled in violin and the ukulele. (Yep, that little guitar often heard in Hawaiian music.)

Logan taught himself to play several instruments, including the bass guitar (SHOWN HERE).

The ever-creative Logan wrote his own songs too. As Emma Watson, another *Perks* star, would later gush, Logan became "the most incredible" musician.

## An Awesome Learning Experience

In 2004, Logan made his debut in a TV series—a WB drama called *Jack & Bobby*. Logan's character, Bobby, was a lot like Charlie in *Perks*. And critics raved about Logan's performance of

DEBUT =
*an actor's first appearance in a particular medium, such as TV*

the teen misfit. The show didn't catch on, though. *Jack & Bobby* was dropped in its second season.

Logan attends a WB party with *Jack & Bobby* actors Christine Lahti (CENTER) and Matt Long (RIGHT).

Looking back, Logan is so grateful for *Jack & Bobby*. He learned a ton. His passion grew beyond acting to include the whole process of producing a show.

Logan also met fellow actor Dean Collins on set. Dean was just as obsessed with movies as Logan was!

## AWKWARD!

Logan puckered up for his first on-screen kiss for *Jack & Bobby*. Twelve-year-old Logan had to lock lips with a nineteen-year-old actress. It was "so awkward," Logan says. (His later on-screen kisses went *much* better!)

Logan became a better actor when working on *Jack & Bobby*.

Logan shared his passion for moviemaking with his best friend, Dean Collins (LEFT).

The BFFs also shared a twisted sense of humor. Soon Dean and Logan were creating their own bursts of movie magic. They wrote, edited, directed, and starred in short films they posted on YouTube.

Logan laughs about those old videos now. He wouldn't exactly call them great art. But they gave the budding film geek the hands-on experience he craved.

## FIVE RANDOM LOGAN FACTS

1. He's a slob.
2. He always travels with a musical instrument.
3. His longest relationship was two years.
4. One of his dreams is to have kids someday.
5. He hates watching himself on-screen and being interviewed.

Logan sees Jim Carrey (RIGHT) as a role model.

CHAPTER TWO

# "THE MOVIE GUY"

Logan and Dean Collins (RIGHT) don't take themselves too seriously when it comes to making movies.

*Fifteen-year-old Logan Lerman looks worried. He's wandering through his big, empty house. Cue creepy music … then footsteps … and a blackout.*

*Next shot: Logan's tied to a chair, gagged. His eyes are wide with fear. The door opens, and Dean Collins saunters in. "You're a big movie star now, right? You work with ALL your big name actors," Dean taunts his friend.*

*"You don't think I read the YouTube comments?" Dean's voice gets high and creepy. "Logan's so hot. Logan, I love your face structure! I love your blue eyes!" Dean starts doing psycho karate moves while Logan shakes with terror …*

Logan and Dean's short movie "Jealousy" ends with Dean punching Logan out. It's not exactly based on a true story. Still, it captures a time in Logan's life.

## Logan's Playground

By 2007, Logan had been in films with huge stars. They included Christian Bale, Russell Crowe, and Ashton Kutcher.

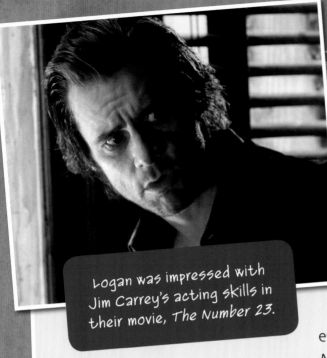

Logan was impressed with Jim Carrey's acting skills in their movie, *The Number 23*.

Most often, Logan played a son or a younger version of the male lead.

Logan loved watching Hollywood's best actors at work. That was especially true for *The Number 23*, with Jim Carrey. To this day, Logan models his own acting style on Carrey's, he says.

A big part of that style is experimentation. Logan might try the same line six different ways. For Logan, a movie set is like a playground. The better the other actors are, the bigger the playground. They catch whatever Logan throws and make it interesting.

## A FOOL FOR ACTING

Before he can experiment, Logan needs to feel comfortable. He has a special trick for getting there. "It helps me to yell or look like an idiot on set," he says. "So when I'm about to do a scene, I've already embarrassed myself."

## Nerdy Cool

As a teen, Logan felt as though he had two separate lives. He'd shoot movies for a month or two. Then it was back to life at Beverly Hills High School.

No doubt, Loggie was superpopular in high school, right? Well, not exactly. **"I was just the movie guy,"** Logan says. He reports that he was somewhere between "cool and nerdy." He mostly hung with a small group of tight friends.

As for how he did in class … Logan admits he didn't pay much attention to his teachers. He was too busy trying out characters, either in his head or with his friends. After school, Logan went to the movies or he shot videos with Dean.

Logan wasn't Mr. Popularity at Beverly Hills High (BELOW), but he was happy to have friends who shared his love of movies.

Mick Jagger from the Rolling Stones—
one of Logan's favorite bands

The guys also
played in the band Indigo
with another friend. They created their own wacky sound.
Logan jammed on guitar and keyboard. Meanwhile,
Dean yelped lyrics like "Tomato, tomato, avocado! Potato,
potato, Rosie O'Donnell!"

## Half-Blood Hero

In 2009, Logan landed the lead in *Percy Jackson & the
Olympians: The Lightning Thief*. Logan spent months
reading Greek myths to play Percy, the half-human son
of Poseidon. He figured out how to do a Brooklyn accent
and invented a new walk. **"I didn't want to play myself
being Percy,"** he explained.

Meanwhile, he trained like crazy. He learned
kickboxing, martial arts, and sword fighting. He practiced
"flying" on wire rigs. Scuba lessons were also key.

In one scene, Percy just sits at the bottom of a pool. Logan had to learn to do that without panicking.

*Percy* was Logan's first big action movie. A lot of Logan's scenes were in front of a green screen. Computer-animated characters would be added later.

Many actors complain about green screen work. Logan admits it feels weird pretending to fight something that isn't there. But mostly, he sees it as another way to flex his imagination.

## GO AHEAD, HIT HIM

Logan says on-screen combat is really hard. You have to feel totally comfortable with your opponent. Logan's first stage fight ever was for *Percy*, against actress Alexandra Daddario. The only problem was that Logan and Alex didn't know each other very well yet. So Logan found a quick way to make sure Alex wouldn't hold back. He told her he was wearing padding—even though he wasn't. Ouch!

PERCY JACKSON & OLYMPIANS
THE LIGHTNING THIEF

Wielding swords in *The Three Musketeers* are (LEFT TO RIGHT) Ray Stevenson, Matthew Macfadyen, Logan, and Luke Evans.

# CHAPTER THREE

# THE PERKS OF STARDOM

Logan signs posters with costar Alexandra Daddario for *Percy Jackson: Sea of Monsters.*

Percy Jackson changed things for Logan. All of a sudden, studio bosses were handing him roles. In June 2010, Logan graduated from Beverly Hills High. That fall, he began playing one of the most famous characters of all time. He was D'Artagnan in *The Three Musketeers*, and he didn't even have to audition.

## A Huge Honor

Logan had a personal reason for taking the part. In the 1930s, Logan's grandfather Max Lerman was a Jewish child living in Nazi Germany. Max and his family were in grave danger under Nazi leader Adolf Hitler's rule. Soon the time came to flee. Young Max was able to bring just a handful of cherished items. One of those was a book—*The Three Musketeers*.

Logan tried growing out his locks for D'Artagnan, but he just got a big fro. That meant hair extensions. Logan hated his fake hair—especially when it fell out at restaurants! He sported his awkward do for a full five months.

Logan had thought training for *Percy* was hard. But this training made that look like theater camp. Logan's character is a highly skilled French sword fighter. So Logan's sword fights were incredibly complex. Plus, the stage swords were made of real metal—that sent real sparks flying!

Logan says he treats every set like his personal film school. That was especially true this time. *Musketeers* was shot in real 3-D. The cameras were awesome! All kinds of movie professionals buzzed around the set. Logan was like a shadow, following them around. He even came on his days off to find out more about their jobs.

REAL 3-D = technology that makes sharper 3-D images than when a 2-D movie is just made into 3-D

## Digging Deep

Logan's next role was a huge change of pace. Logan wouldn't have to do dangerous stunts to play Charlie in *The Perks of Being a Wallflower*. But the difficult role scared him plenty. Still, Logan just had an **"indescribable passion"** to play sweet, messed-up Charlie.

Logan knew he had to connect with Charlie's pain to bring the character to life. So Logan looked for ways to shake up his mental state. Isolating himself was big. Watching disturbing documentaries also helped. Logan watched more than fifty films of real people in real pain. He was particularly shaken by *Gladiator Days: Anatomy of a Prison Murder*. He thought of that movie during one scene where Charlie breaks down from images running through his head.

DOCUMENTARIES =
__movies about true events__

Perks costar Mae Whitman shows off a magazine with Logan's face on it. He is certainly famous!

HARDEST SCENE FOR LOGAN: when Charlie has a breakdown

MOST EMBARRASSING SCENE: singing along to *The Rocky Horror Picture Show* in a golden thong

FAVORITE SCENE: the "Truth or Dare?" sequence

Logan and Emma Watson (LEFT) get some advice for a scene from *Perks* director Stephen Chbosky.

Another challenge for Logan was mapping out Charlie's "arc." He needed to understand how Charlie changes over the course of the story. Like most movies, though, *Perks* wasn't filmed in order. That didn't help! Logan's solution was to figure out Charlie's "intention" in every scene. If Logan understood what Charlie wanted in that particular moment, the scene would work.

## More Open Doors

When *Perks* wrapped, Logan wasn't exhausted just from the work. He'd also spent way too many late nights jamming with his costars, including Emma Watson. They'd formed a band they called Octopus Jam. Logan wrote original music for the band. He also wrote a special song for each of his cast mates.

Thanks to Charlie, Logan earned new respect as a serious actor. His work on *Perks* landed him a choice role in the movie *Noah*, about the famous Bible figure. Logan couldn't believe he had enough actor cred to work with award-winning director Darren Aronofsky.

Filming for *Noah* would start in summer 2012. In the meantime, Logan went back into Greek god mode for *Percy Jackson: Sea of Monsters*. The twenty-year-old actor was stoked to be swinging a sword again. **"I'm still a kid,"** he explained with a shrug. Plus, the sequel had some epic monsters.

What's next for Logan? He's signed on for one more Percy movie. In 2014, fans will also see him in *Fury*, a World War II thriller with Brad Pitt. For now, Logan's on the lookout for more great roles with great directors.

But mark his words. He *will* be sitting in the director's chair someday. **"Almost the only thing I want to do in my life is make movies,"** Logan says. No doubt, this film geek has the passion, talent, and determination to make that dream come true.

Logan attends a Sea of Monsters event.

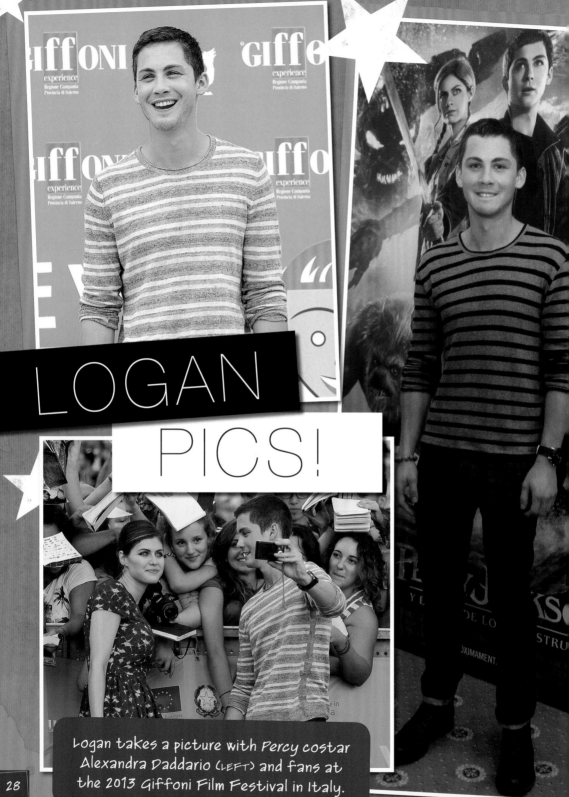

# LOGAN
## PICS!

Logan takes a picture with *Percy* costar
Alexandra Daddario (LEFT) and fans at
the 2013 Giffoni Film Festival in Italy.

Logan plays with a new young friend he made at the 2012 Working Dreams and Families for Children holiday celebration.

Logan celebrated the premiere of *Percy Jackson & The Olympians: The Lightning Thief* with the cast at the top of the Empire State Building.

5.    "The Insider: Logan Lerman," *Nylon Guys*, August 9, 2011, http://www.nylonmag.com/?section=article&parid=6692.

6.    "'Perks of Being a Wallflower's' Logan Lerman Graces Fault Magazine," *International Business Times*, October 18, 2012, http://au.ibtimes.com/articles/395665/20121018/logan-lerman-perks-being-wallflower-flaunt-magazine.htm#.UcNcP9isKYw.

6.    Jenelle Riley, "A Wall Flower Takes the Lead," *Back Stage*, September 16, 2012, 18.

7.    "Interview: Logan Lerman (The Perks of Being a Wallflower)," *Flixist*, November 29, 2012, http://www.flixist.com/interview-logan-lerman-the-perks-of-being-a-wallflower--213854.phtml.

9.    Logan Lerman, Twitter post, nd, https://twitter.com/LoganLerman.

9.    "Logan Lerman Interview on Bonnie Hunt Show 02/17," YouTube video, 6:10, posted by Logan Lerman, February 17, 2010, https://www.youtube.com/watch?v=HQTsdsY4guc.

11.   "Logan Lerman," Hulu video, 4:26, nd, http://www.hulu.com/watch/408822.

13.   "Emma Watson: 'Logan Is the Most Incredible Piano Player,'" YouTube video, 0:42, posted by Anderson, September 17, 2012, http://www.youtube.com/watch?NR=1&feature=endscreen&v=EGlGDOyyhbo.

14.   "Logan Lerman Emma Watson Wasn't My First Onscreen Kiss 8th October 2012," YouTube video, 5:38, posted by CelebritiesInterview, November 2, 2012, http://www.youtube.com/watch?v=wP6iKz83bQk.

17.   "Jealousy," YouTube video, 4:09, posted by monkeynuts1069, July 26, 2007, https://www.youtube.com/watch?v=YhjVrtu1iAs.

17.   Ibid.

18.   Jim Windolf, "Logan Lerman: The Quadruple Threat," *Vanity Fair*, January 2010, http://www.vanityfair.com/hollywood/features/2010/01/logan-lerman-slideshow-201001.

19.   "Logan Lerman Emma Watson Wasn't My First Onscreen Kiss," YouTube.

20.   "Touch Screen," Indigo, *MySpace.com*, accessed June 20, 2013, https://myspace.com/weareindigo/music/song/touch-screen-64380912-70467434.

20.   "Logan Lerman on ABC News Radio," YouTube video, 7:04, posted by Sarah Sweeney, February 9, 2010, http://www.youtube.com/watch?v=sQM4sfrhHTE.

25.   Edward Douglas, "Oscar-Worthy: Logan Lerman on Perks, Percy & Noah," *ComingSoon.net*, December 7, 2012, http://www.comingsoon.net/news/weekendwarriornews.php?id=97784.

27.   "Sneak Peek: 'Percy Jackson: Sea of Monsters,'" *USA Today*, March 21, 2013, http://www.usatoday.com/story/life/movies/2013/03/21/percy-jackson-logan-lerman/2004491/.

27.   Jim Windolf, "I Was a Teenage Demigod," *Vanity Fair*, January 2010, http://www.vanityfair.com/hollywood/features/2010/01/logan-lerman-201001.

# MORE LOGAN INFO

Higgins, Nadia. *Emma Watson: From Wizards to Wallflowers*. Minneapolis: Lerner Publications, 2014. Get the inside scoop on Logan's *Perks* costar and one of his biggest fans.

Logan's Twitter Feed
https://twitter.com/LoganLerman
Check out Logan's feed for movie recommendations and links to short films. Once in a while, he posts news about himself.

MySpace: Indigo
http://www.myspace.com/weareindigo
Listen to samples by Logan and Dean's high-school band, Indigo.

*Perks*' Tumblr Site
http://wallflowermovie.tumblr.com
Remember favorite quotes and scenes from *The Perks of Being a Wallflower*. It's like a scrapbook about Charlie, Sam, and Patrick.

YouTube: Monkeynuts1069 channel
http://www.youtube.com/user/monkeynuts1069
See Logan's more zany side in "Scouts," "Jealousy," and other short videos. He and BFF Dean Collins made these off-the-wall shorts back in high school.

# INDEX